W9-AGG-002

BUILDING

AMERICA

The Seattle Space Needle

Craig A. Doherty and Katherine M. Doherty

A BLACKBIRCH PRESS BOOK

WOODBRIDGE, CONNECTICUT

To the memory of our friend, Donna Campbell

Special Thanks

The publisher would like to thank Stephanie LaBrie and K. Russ Goodman of the Space Needle Corporation; Carolyn J. Marr of the Seattle Museum of History and Industry; Pam Dotson of The Seattle Times; and Dennis Barrow of Otis Elevator Company for their valuable help and cooperation on this project.

Published by Blackbirch Press, Inc.
260 Amity Road
Woodbridge, CT 06525

© 1997 Blackbirch Press, Inc.
First Edition

Printed in the United States

10 9 8 7 6 5 4 3 2 1

Editorial Director: Bruce Glassman
Senior Editor: Nicole Bowen
Associate Editor: Elizabeth M. Taylor
Design and Production: Moore Graphics!

Photo Credits

Cover and title page: Courtesy of Space Needle Corporation; contents page (from top to bottom): ©Mike Howell/Leo de Wys, Inc.; Special Collections Division, University of Washington Libraries; Johny Closs/*Seattle Times*; Museum of History and Industry; Page 4: ©Mike Howell/Leo de Wys, Inc.; page 6: ©Bill Bachman/Leo de Wys, Inc.; pages 8, 23: *Seattle Times*; page 10: Larry Dion/*Seattle Times*; pages 12, 16: Special Collections Division, University of Washington Libraries; page 15: AP/Wide World Photos; pages 18, 27, 32, 35, 36: Museum of History and Industry; page 19: Otis Elevator Company Historic Archives; pages 20, 26: Johny Closs/*Seattle Times*; page 25: John Graham Associates/DLR Group; pages 29, 40, 42–43: Courtesy of Space Needle Corporation; page 34: Ben Benschneider/*Seattle Times*; page 38: Ron DeRosa/*Seattle Times*; page 39: Jim Bates/*Seattle Times*.

Library of Congress Cataloging-in-Publication Data

Doherty, Craig A.
    The Seattle Space Needle / by Craig A. Doherty and Katherine M. Doherty.—1st ed.
        p. cm.—(Building America)
    Includes bibliographical references and index.
    Summary: Discusses the history of the structure built for the 1962 Seattle World's Fair, describing the engineering, architectural, and mechanical processes involved.
    ISBN 1-56711-114-9 (lib. binding:alk. paper)
    1. Space Needle (Seattle, Wash.)—History—Juvenile literature. 2. Towers—Washington (State)—Seattle—Design and construction—Juvenile literature. [1. Space Needle (Seattle, Wash.) 2. Towers—Design and construction.] I. Doherty, Katherine M. II. Title. III. Series: Doherty, Craig A. Building America.
    TA660.T6D65 1997   95-39085
    725'.97'09797772—dc20   CIP
                                                             AC

Table of Contents

Introduction

Seattle is the largest city in the state of Washington. It is situated in an area of great natural beauty, surrounded by lakes, mountains, and Puget Sound. Since its founding in 1852, the city has become an important center of shipping and manufacturing in the Northwest. Seattle was originally inhabited by the Suquamish and Snohomish Indians, and the city was named after the Suquamish chief Seatlh. After World War II, Seattle grew to a population of more than 500,000 people due in part to the presence of Boeing and other aerospace-technology companies. In the late 1950s, a group of residents wanted to show off their city by hosting a world's fair. As plans proceeded for the fair, it was decided that a center-piece, which would stand as a symbol of Seattle long after the fair was over, was needed. The symbol they came up with was the Space Needle.

The Space Needle is a towering 605-foot structure with a restaurant and observation deck that seem to float above the Seattle landscape. At the time it was built, it was an engineering marvel and the tallest structure west of the Mississippi River. Today, it continues to operate as a restaurant and tourist attraction, and, despite being more than 30 years old, still looks like a design for the twenty-first century.

Opposite:
The glowing lights of the Space Needle's tophouse make it resemble a flying saucer against the nighttime sky.

1

A Symbol of Seattle

 Century 21 Exposition, Inc. was formed in 1955 after a favorable vote by the people of Seattle. The purpose of Century 21 was to organize and put on a world class exposition in Seattle. At first, the organizers thought they would host a fair that celebrated the 50th anniversary of the very success-ful Alaska-Yukon-Pacific Exposition held in 1909. Then, in 1957, the Soviet Union launched the first space satellite—called *Sputnik*—and many people in the United States became concerned with winning the "space race" against the Soviets.

*Opposite:
The "space race"
helped inspire
the Seattle
Space Needle's
futuristic look.*

Edward Carlson, the president of Western Hotels, (right) and Joseph Gandy, president of the Seattle World's Fair, both worked to make the Space Needle a reality.

The organizers realized they would never be able to put on a quality fair by 1959. They also realized that the sudden increased interest in science might be the key to generate enthusiasm for a world's fair in Seattle. Edward Carlson, the president of the Western Hotel chain, had been appointed head of Century 21. He and others had been successful in getting the state legislature to promise $10 million for the fair. They also got a commitment of $7.5 million from the city of Seattle, and, when they chose science as the theme, the U.S. Congress agreed to provide $9 million for a U.S. science pavillion at the fair.

Once Carlson had lined up the money from the local, state, and federal governments, the fair

Say CHEESE

When the Soviet Union launched the first human-made satellite, *Sputnik*, on October 4, 1957, Americans rushed out into their backyards to see it, and they became concerned that the Soviets might have a tactical advantage in space. *Sputnik* was in part responsible for the Seattle World's Fair's theme of science and technology, and it also spurred the United States to spend billions of dollars on its own space program. When the fair opened in 1962, four Americans and two Soviets had made journeys into orbit, and many people became interested in the possibilities of space travel.

Some people believe that if we are able to send people and unmanned spacecraft to the moon and beyond, then other beings living in distant solar systems might be able to travel to Earth. Some people claim to have seen spacecraft from other worlds and to have met aliens. So far, none of these stories have been proven, however, one group believes that the Space Needle was built as part of an attempt to contact advanced beings in other solar systems.

The Committee Hoping for Extra-terrestrial Encounters to Save the Earth (CHEESE) has stated that they have a copy of secret plans that prove the Space Needle was not built as a restaurant and tourist attraction. They claim the plans show that the Space Needle is really a specially designed antenna that is being used to make contact with advanced beings in other solar systems. If this were true, then the disc jockeys and others who have broadcast from the Space Needle would give the idea of a universal audience a whole new meaning!

In addition to CHEESE's interest in the Space Needle, other UFO (unidentified-flying-object) and science-fiction fans have shown an interest in it. In 1966, the Space Needle hosted a "skywatch" for flying saucers, and in 1968, a couple that was very interested in UFOs was married there. In 1978, when Seattle hosted the second annual science-fiction exposition, the operators of the Space Needle used special lighting effects to make the Space Needle look like a spaceship hovering in the Seattle sky.

president, Joseph E. Gandy, went to Paris, France, to meet with the Bureau of International Expositions, which had been set up to grant sites the right to host a world's fair. The bureau approved Seattle's plan, and what had started out to be a celebration

Space-themed exhibits were common at the Seattle World's Fair. Here fairgoers watch planets flash by during a simulated space journey.

of Seattle's place in the history of the Northwest became the 1962 Seattle World's Fair.

Ultimately, 40 foreign countries and more than 400 companies participated in the fair. The Japanese built a replica of a Japanese village, while the tiny country of San Marino displayed its special postage stamps. Many other countries displayed items unique to their people. The plans also included a new civic center and theaters that would remain there after the fair for the betterment of Seattle. The technology theme was played out in exhibit after exhibit, however, the organizers of the event wanted to create a centerpiece for the fair. Even after they came up with the idea for a "space needle," there were many problems that still had to be solved in the designing and building of such an innovative structure.

The Idea on a Napkin

In 1959, Edward Carlson was in Stuttgart, Germany, an old European city that had been partially destroyed during World War II. In rebuilding Stuttgart, architects had blended some of the most modern architecture with medieval castles and the other remaining old sections of the city. Standing above all of this was a television broadcast tower that included a restaurant from which visitors could view the city. It has been reported that while Carlson sat in the Stuttgart tower restaurant, he sketched a similar structure on a napkin.

Carlson supposedly sent a postcard of the tower to Ewen Dingwall, the person hired to manage the fair, and wrote on the back, "Why not something like this for the fair?" He also brought back to Seattle the napkin with the sketch that looked like a flying saucer on a tripod. Many thought it was a great idea, and they decided to see if a plan could be devised to build a tower for the fair.

On to the Architects

Carlson and other fair organizers went to the Seattle offices of architect Jack Graham to see if their idea of a tower for the fair was feasible. Graham agreed to have people in his Seattle office work up some preliminary sketches, realizing that at this point he was working on speculation and there was no promise that his company would be hired to design and build anything. Graham was a good choice because his firm had recently designed a revolving restaurant for the top of an office building in the Ala Moana Shopping Center in Honolulu, Hawaii.

In the early stages, a variety of shapes for the Seattle tower were tried and rejected. Some plans were not what the organizers wanted visually, while others presented impossible engineering problems. One that the designers liked looked like a balloon held to the ground by a series of interwoven cables. The fair people, however, kept returning to the simplicity of Carlson's original idea—something like a spaceship on a pedestal. John Ridley at Graham's office did most of the preliminary work on the tower, but, when the designers there ran into difficulties

There were many early designs for the Seattle tower—some quite different from the final building.

coming up with a good approach, they turned for help to Victor Steinbrueck, a noted University of Washington architecture professor.

It has been reported that John Ridley thought of the design that would eventually become the Space Needle while on vacation. He conceived of a central tower leading to a saucer-shaped structure, all of which would be supported by three exterior legs. Steinbrueck, after consulting with others at the university, also decided that a three-legged design would be the most practical. Both Steinbrueck and Ridley saw their designs using some form of reinforced concrete for the sloping legs of the tower.

By now, it was early 1960 and the fair was only two years away. Time was becoming a real problem if the Space Needle was going to be ready for the fair. Time, however, was not the only problem. The concrete experts that Ridley, Steinbrueck, and others talked to could not agree on how to build the structure. Some thought that the concrete should be poured on site using slip forms that could be moved up the legs as they worked. Others thought that the legs should be made of huge panels of prestressed concrete that could be fabricated at a cement plant and then brought to the site and assembled.

The architects and engineers finally decided that there was too much uncertainty dealing with concrete. Steel manufacturers had assured the designers that the tower could be built of steel. The decision was made to go with steel, and the designers worked furiously to complete the plans. By the time the final plans were approved, it was the fall of 1960 and there was only a year and a half left to actually build the Space Needle.

Finding a Site, Finding the Money

While Graham's firm wrestled with the design, Carlson, Gandy, and others dealt with the problems of funding the project and locating an acceptable site within the fairgrounds. The Space Needle would have to be built somewhere on the site of the fair, and much of the land had been bought by the city for a civic center. Many at Century 21 and in the city government were concerned that there might be legal problems if the city leased some of the land earmarked for the civic center to a private concern.

The deeds for all the land that the fair was to use were carefully studied. It was discovered that the city owned a 120-foot-square plot near the middle of the fairgrounds that was not part of the civic center parcel. This land contained switching equipment for the fire-and-police alarm system of the city. After the land was tested and found to be suitable, it was sold to the newly formed Space Needle Corporation.

The Space Needle Corporation was created because it was impossible to build the tower with public money. Gandy had tried to get the King County commissioners to pay for the construction with public funds, but they had refused to take the question to the voters. Many were skeptical about investing in a restaurant that would appear to float 500 feet above the city. At that time, Joseph Gandy traveled to Stuttgart, Germany, and was given the opportunity to examine the financial books for the Stuttgart tower. He saw that it was economically successful. He also went to Tokyo, Japan, where he learned that their tower—which is similar to France's Eiffel Tower—was also financially a success.

With these optimistic facts from Stuttgart and Tokyo, Gandy and Carlson were able to get enough investors and—even more important—convinced the banks to loan them the money for the construction of the Space Needle. The way was now clear to build, but time was extremely short.

Joseph Gandy (left) meets with businessmen to discuss fair plans. A model of the Space Needle can be seen behind them.

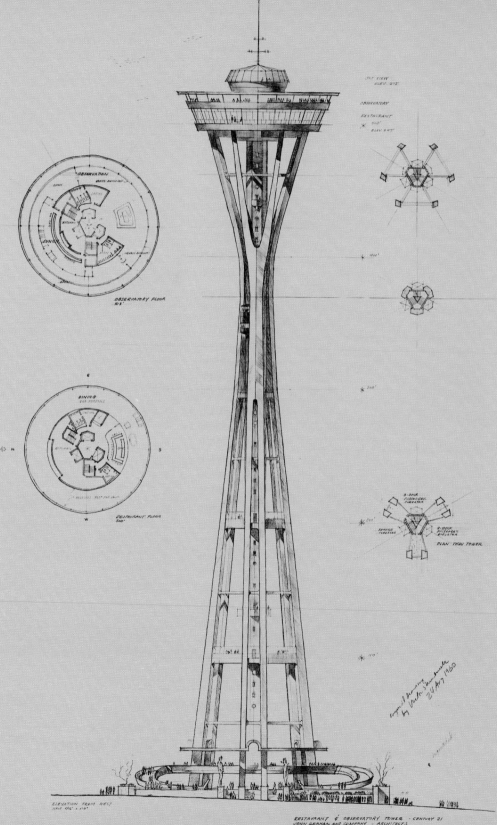

ELEVATION FROM WEST

RESTAURANT & OBSERVATORY TOWER - CENTURY 21
JOHN GRAHAM AND COMPANY - ARCHITECTS

2

Building a Base

After testing the soil to be sure that the structure's foundation would be stable, work began on the excavation. The first power-shovel full of dirt was removed from the site on April 17, 1961, and workers for Howard S. Wright Constructors kept the trucks, bulldozers, and shovels running for 11 days. At the end of that time, the workers had created a hole 30 feet deep that covered the entire 120-foot-square site.

You Have to Dig Down, Before You Can Build Up

One of the most important aspects of engineering the Space Needle was lowering the center of gravity. The lower the center of gravity, the more stable the slender tower and its saucerlike top would be. The

Opposite: Many architectural drawings were done during the design process. This one shows plans for the different levels of the tophouse.

17

ideal situation would be to have the center of gravity for the tower at or just below ground level. The designers were able to accomplish that by making the below-ground foundation weigh more than the entire above-ground structure. It was also hoped that, even if the Space Needle moved during an earthquake or other natural disaster, it would end up standing straight up because of the low center of gravity.

Filling in the Hole

After digging the hole, the construction workers laid more than 250 tons of steel reinforcing bars—called rebar—into the base of the foundation. In addition

This model shows the ultramodern structures and landscape planned for the fairgrounds.

to the rebar, 96 massive anchor bolts had to be precisely placed before the concrete could be poured. The steel workers would then attach the steel tower and legs to these bolts. The central tower of the Space Needle required 24 anchor bolts 3 inches in diameter and 12 feet long. Each of the 3 outer legs would also require 24 anchor bolts; the leg bolts were 32 feet long and 4 inches in diameter. The large bolts on the legs were needed to withstand the greater forces that the legs were expected to exert.

Pouring the Concrete

When the cement trucks began to roll early in the morning on May 26, 1961, they began what was, at the time, the largest continuous pour of concrete in history. The first truck started pouring at 5:00 A.M., and, 12 hours later, the trucks had pulled up to the hole 467 times and dumped their loads. At times, there were as many as eight trucks dumping concrete into the foundation at once. Down in the hole, people worked furiously to keep up with the flow. The concrete had to be spread evenly and then compacted into place using power vibrators. At the end of the day, 5,850 tons of concrete had been poured into the foundation— enough to fill seven five-room houses from floor to ceiling!

The foundation had to be completed before the steel work could begin.

Twenty-first-Century Tower

On March 30, 1961, the first orders for the steel went out to U.S. Steel; they called for the largest I-shaped beams that the company was capable of making. The order specified that the long side of the I be 36 inches, while the top and bottom flanges were to be 17 inches wide. The steel was to be 1¾ inches thick. The giant blast furnaces at U.S. Steel poured out an ingot that weighed 28,000 pounds. It was rolled out into one 27,000-pound beam, 90 feet long.

Opposite:
The Space Needle's innovative design made its construction a true engineering challenge.

21

To form the steel for the legs, three of these beams were welded together and reinforced with a series of steel baffles. When the welders were finished, they had a 90-foot section of one of the legs that weighed 90,000 pounds. (The total weight of the steel that went into the construction of the Space Needle was 3,700 tons.) By the time they had finished, the welders had used more than 146,500 pounds of welding rods to fabricate the steel sections of the Space Needle.

To make certain that the welds had been done according to the specifications, the work was carefully inspected. All the butt welds that were under tension in the structure were radiographed ("photographed" with radio waves) according to standards set up by the American Society of Mechanical Engineers (ASME). The ASME code called for 20 percent of other welds to be checked as well. All the quality checks met or exceeded the ASME code. The steel that was 1¾ inches thick or less was checked by X ray, while thicker steel required a special machine that used iridium 90 and had the equivalent power of a 400,000-volt X-ray machine.

One of the most difficult aspects of constructing the Space Needle was bending the steel so that it would curve into the central tower 373 feet above the ground and then flare back out to support the restaurant and observation levels. At first, the engineers were puzzled about how this would be accomplished. The steel workers at Pacific Car and Foundry—the steel-erection contractor on the project—had recently completed a job where steel beams that had been bent in a fire were straightened by heating them and bending them back into shape. They felt that the same could be done with the Space Needle's legs, only in reverse. They would take the straight beams, heat them with welding torches, and then bend them into shape on a large jig, or pattern.

Up to the Sky

With all the engineering problems solved, the first steel was lowered onto the giant anchor bolts and attached with equally massive nuts in June 1961. The last nut needed to be tightened down by early December 1961. To many, it seemed an impossible task, however, the workers of Pacific Car and Foundry were up to the challenge. They began on the central core tower that was to include two sets of stairs and all the pipes, wires, and cables for the elevators and other mechanical systems that would be needed above. The three elevators, made by Otis Elevator, would run on the outside of the central tower— one on each of the tower's three sides. At first, it was easy to erect the central tower using ground-based cranes. The engineers knew, however, that they would quickly build up out of the reach of even the tallest crane.

Paul Collop designed a special crane that could climb the Space Needle as the tower was built.

To solve this problem, Paul Collop, the erection superintendent, designed a special crane that would fit inside the central tower. Not only would the crane be able to lift the 90,000-pound leg sections, it would also be able to lift itself up as the tower was built around it. As the crane climbed the tower, the workers were not quite sure how they would get the crane down once it reached the top!

The most dangerous job for the steel workers was bolting the sections of the legs together. Two 90-foot sections of a leg were joined together with three splice plates of 1¾-inch steel. Each plate had as many as 120 bolt holes that corresponded to holes in the ends of the beams. It took two workers to place and tighten the 360 bolts at the junction of two leg sections. One worker would be inside the tube created by the three welded beams, the other would be hanging from the steel or standing in a metal box held up by a crane. These metal boxes, called skips, were used to transport workers and materials to the places where they were needed.

The construction crew had to work closely and communicate well with each other. The tools they used weighed more than 50 pounds and were operated by 100 pounds of air pressure. If one worker let go of his or her tool without telling his or her partner, the partner's tool could spin danger-ously. One man who almost caused a serious accident by not telling his partner that he was letting go was sent immediately to the ground and fired. There had been no serious accidents on the Space Needle, and the people in charge of the workers wanted to keep it that way.

Between June and December 1961, the Space Needle
grew quickly to tower over the Seattle skyline.

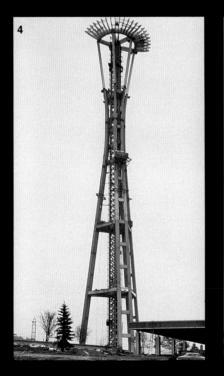

Decorative steel rays had to be put in place before the tophouse's floor could be built.

Building the "Flying Saucer"

By September 1, 1961, the steel tower had reached 200 feet, and it looked like Pacific Car and Foundry would be on schedule. After the 373-foot level, the three outer legs split to provide six outer supporting points for the restaurant and observation deck at the 500-foot level. The ring of steel that was to support the restaurant came up in 40,000-pound pieces that had been prefabricated on the ground. The pieces included the decorative rays that jut out from the base of the restaurant level and look like the rays of the sun.

Once the floor of the restaurant level was in, the rest of the tophouse could be constructed. The building on the top of the Space Needle is largest on the second level, which is the observation area. This level is 515 feet above the ground and has a circumference of 350 feet. One of the most difficult and dangerous aspects of constructing the Space Needle was attaching the sun louvers, which extend outward

Workers raced to finish the construction of the tophouse before the winter of 1961–62 set in.

at the base of the observation deck. The crane in the central tower could not reach out to the tip of the sun louvers, and the last ring of 75-pound pieces had to be set by hand. With nothing to stand on or hold onto, the workers inched their way out the half-foot-wide, downward-sloping steel "rays" and hung out over 515 feet of air as they bolted the pieces into place. Work had to be stopped when it began to snow one day in November. Despite the shortness of time, the difficulty of the job, and the unpredictable weather of the Northwest, the steel work for the Space Needle was completed on time.

The crane lifted all the materials up to the tophouse. Completing the tophouse of the Space Needle was similar to constructing other buildings of that size. The design provided for offices, restrooms, the heating and air-conditioning machinery, the elevator equipment, the kitchens, and a gift shop, as well as the restaurants and observation level. The major difference was the altitude of the job, there aren't many other buildings whose first floor is 500 feet above the ground!

One unusual feature of the Space Needle is the rotating restaurant, which is actually a narrow outer band of the restaurant level. Behind the restaurant are the food preparation areas and a lobby. The floor of the restaurant is on tracks and is driven by a one-horsepower electric motor—about the power of a household vacuum cleaner! It takes the restaurant a total of 58 minutes to make one complete rotation. Those who eat dinner in the Space Needle get to see all 360 degrees of the view of Seattle and the surrounding countryside without leaving their seats.

There are actually five levels in the tophouse of the Space Needle. In addition to the two public areas, there are two levels above the observation deck that house the mechanical equipment needed to operate the structure. Between the restaurant and the observation deck is a level that holds administrative offices and additional kitchen space.

The roof of the Space Needle has its own unique features, such as the 50-foot-tall torch tower. This was the last piece to be lifted into place. It was designed to include a gas flame that would burn in the base, while the top of the tower would serve as a navigational aid for aircraft in the area and as the topmost lightning rod. There are 24 other rods that ring the roof and protect the Space Needle from lightning bolts.

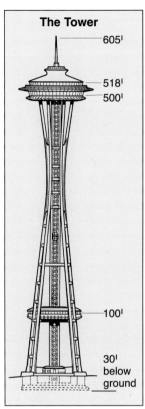

The Tower

- 605'
- 518'
- 500'
- 100'
- 30' below ground

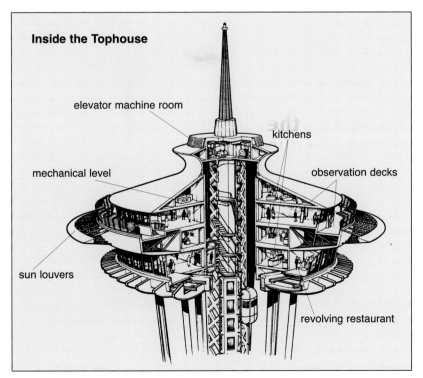

Inside the Tophouse

elevator machine room

kitchens

mechanical level

observation decks

sun louvers

revolving restaurant

Top: The Space Needle's observation decks are at an elevation of 518 feet. The revolving restaurant is 500 feet above the ground. **Bottom:** The tophouse has five levels, but only two are open to the public.

STRUCK BY LIGHTNING

Each year lightning kills about 100 people in the United States, which is more than die in hurricanes and tornadoes combined. Lightning is the discharge of electricity built up in rain clouds. Sometimes the discharge is from cloud to cloud, and other times it comes down from the clouds and strikes the Earth. Scientists disagree on how lightning is caused, but all agree that when lightning strikes, it carries an extremely dangerous charge of electricity.

Benjamin Franklin, a signer of the Declaration of Independence and an inventor, devised the first lightning rod to protect houses. A lightning rod is a metal rod placed on the highest point of a building and connected to the ground by a wire. The rod attracts the electricity by giving it an easy route to the ground. Thanks to Franklin's 1760 invention, tall structures such as the Space Needle can be protected from lightning.

Many people believe that lightning never strikes the same place twice. The truth, however, is that the tallest structures in an area, such as the Space Needle, are often repeatedly hit by lightning during a single storm. The Space Needle has a ring of 24 lightning rods around the roof of the tophouse and one on top of the torch tower. These are all connected to a large copper ring buried in the ground. Before the tophouse was even finished, the lightning rods were struck during a thunderstorm. It has been reported that the workers inside the building didn't even know that the Space Needle was hit by lightning and just kept on working! Since that first strike, the lightning rods on the Space Needle have been called on to do their job many times.

Lowering the Crane

On December 8, 1961, the crane that Paul Collop had devised to build the Space Needle lifted the 50-foot torch tower onto a temporary rack where it would wait for the crane to be moved out of the way. Collop and the engineers had come up with a plan that they hoped would work. The central tower was left clear from 50 feet below the restaurant level to the top so that the crane could climb back down to the 450-foot level of the structure.

At that point, a section on the tower side had been only temporarily fastened into place and could be removed to let the crane climb out. It took all of the steel workers to help get the 42-ton crane down to the 450-foot level and attempt to swing it out into the air where it could lower itself to the ground. On December 19, 1961, they almost succeeded, but their attempt was defeated by blowing rain and sleet.

The next day, the task was completed, and the crane was lowered to the ground. That same day, the steel workers went to the top of the Space Needle and set the torch tower in place. At this point, their job was done. The crew of Howard S. Wright Constructors then had to hurry to complete the finishing work. They had less than four months before the April 21, 1962, opening of the Seattle World's Fair.

Twenty-first-Century Colors

One of the last jobs that had to be done on the Space Needle was painting. The original color scheme called for colors with space-age names. The legs were painted Astronaut White, while the inner core was done in Orbital Olive. The roof and underside of the tophouse were painted Galaxy Gold, and the ribbed halo of sun louvers between the restaurant and the observation deck were painted Re-entry Red. The first painting of the Space Needle required 1,340 gallons of paint. The structure has been repainted a number of times since then, and each repainting requires about 1,000 gallons. The original color scheme was changed in 1968. Today, the Space Needle is only two colors—white and gold.

Space Needle Operation

The World's Fair opened on schedule on April 21, 1962, and the Space Needle was ready. The exposition was a tremendous success, and the Space Needle was one of the most popular attractions. Every morning, 240 hungry people—the capacity of the restaurant—paid six dollars to eat breakfast high above the fair. The six dollars included two dollars for admission to the fair, one dollar for the elevator, and three dollars for breakfast. It has been estimated that nearly 20,000 people a day paid one dollar for adults and 75 cents for children to ride the elevators to the observation level. The Space Needle's manager at the time, Hoge Sullivan, estimated that 2.75 million people rode the elevators during the fair.

Opposite: *The 1962 Seattle World's Fair was a great success. It was one of the few World's Fairs that made a profit.*

Many of those people bought some of the more than 200 souvenirs created for the Seattle World's Fair. The two most popular were a gold charm of the Space Needle that had a light in it and a nine-inch-tall lighter in the shape of the Space Needle. The Space Needle also became an official U.S. post office during the fair, with its own stamp. The post office was dedicated on April 25, 1962, and the first letter went from Senator Warren G. Magnuson of Washington to President John F. Kennedy. The postmark "Space Needle, Washington" was stamped over the fair's commemorative stamp and suggested that President Kennedy "Come to the fair."

The restaurant was leased to Edward Carlson's Western Hotels, which dressed the hostesses in gold coveralls. The outfit was supposed to fit in with the fair's theme of space and the future. By the end of the exhibition, it was obvious that the organizers had made all the right decisions. The Seattle World's Fair was one of only a few world's fairs to make a profit. In fact, the city of Seattle had leased the site for the fair to Century 21 with the understanding that they would only receive rent if there were a profit. The city's six percent of the profits turned into a $975,000 windfall.

One of the fair's most popular souvenirs was a Space Needle lighter (center).

"Transportation of the Future"

The monorail built for the 1962 World's Fair still runs today.

While the Space Needle was the most-popular attraction of the Seattle World's Fair, the next most popular was the monorail that connected the fairgrounds with downtown Seattle, 1.2 miles away. It was the first monorail in the United States. Lockheed Aircraft Corporation built it using many principles learned in the aircraft industry. The sleek monorail was billed as the "transportation of the future," while, in fact, the idea had been around for more than 100 years.

Although the idea was not new, the construction materials and techniques used in the Seattle monorail were on the cutting edge of technology in 1962. Lockheed built it with high-strength, lightweight materials that were used in the aircraft industry but had never before been applied to ground-based transportation. The monorail cars weigh only 22,000 pounds and carry 94 passengers each. Because the cars are lightweight, the supporting structure could also be less massive than that of other elevated trains.

The monorail in Seattle is built on single supports spaced 85 feet apart. Two tracks run along the supports, allowing monorail cars to travel in both directions at the same time. The cars are fueled by electricity, are more powerful than any other monorail in the United States, and carry the most passengers. Today, the monorail runs every 15 minutes from 10:00 A.M. to midnight and connects the old fairgrounds—which have become Seattle Center—to downtown Seattle and the upscale Westlake Mall. People can still ride the monorail to the Space Needle and imagine how impressive these two attractions must have been way back in 1962.

During the fair, approximately 2.75 million people rode the elevators to the top of the Space Needle.

Not only was the fair as a whole profitable, the Space Needle was able to pay back the almost $4 million in building costs. The money came from the elevator fees and the lease of the restaurant to Western Hotels. When the fair closed, the only concern at the Space Needle was whether the landmark would continue to attract visitors without the fair.

From the Fair of Tomorrow to Today

The fair ended on October 21, 1962, and for more than 30 years since that time, the Space Needle has continued to be the most recognizable symbol of Seattle. Year in and year out, it attracts approximately 3,000 visitors a day. More than half of them eat at the costly Emerald Suite or the more moderately priced Space Needle Restaurant on the first level of the tophouse, which together are the ninth-busiest restaurants in the country. In 1994, the readers of *Sunset* magazine voted the Space Needle Restaurant the "best restaurant with a view," and it had five times the votes as the second-place restaurant.

Over the years, the Space Needle has seen it all. A baby was born there in 1974, and a Seattle disc jockey and his wife lived in a small apartment on the

SEATTLE CENTER

After the World's Fair closed, it was time to turn the site into something else. When the plans were made for the fair, the future use of the buildings was considered. The planners envisioned an area that would be used for recreation and entertainment. The result was Seattle Center, which is eclipsed only by Disneyland and Disney World in terms of attendance. More than 5,000 events are scheduled at Seattle Center each year; that's almost 15 events a day!

The 74 acres that had been part of the fair now contain concert halls, sports arenas, restaurants, and shopping areas. In addition, the Fun Forest Amusement Park at Seattle Center offers arcades and rides, and there are also the Seattle Children's Museum and the Pacific Science Center.

In 1990, Seattle Center was the site for the Goodwill Games, and, once again, the city showed that it can host a world-class event.

Elvis Presley (right) starred in It Happened at the World's Fair, *one of several movies shot at the Space Needle.*

observation level for six months. (The disc jockey broadcast his daily show from the Space Needle.) The disc jockey, however, was not the only entertainment that originated from the Space Needle.

In 1981, Larry King, host of a national TV talk show, broadcast from the tower. A number of other local shows have originated from there as well. Over the years, the Space Needle has been featured in a number of movies, including: It *Happened at the World's Fair,* starring Elvis Presley; *Parallax View,* starring Warren Beatty; and *Power,* starring Richard Gere. It's also made appearances in several TV shows, such as "Frasier," "Northern Exposure," and "Twin Peaks."

A number of real-life dramas have been played out at the Space Needle as well. There have been many weddings and other private parties over the years; one group has already booked the Space Needle for a private party on December 31, 1999. It seems that they see the Space Needle as the perfect place to greet the twenty-first century. It has already become the New Year's Eve gathering point for residents of the Northwest. Some have gone as far as to call it the "Times Square of the West." Instead of dropping a ball at midnight, the Space Needle's lights are turned out and then turned back on slowly,

Celebrating New Year's Eve at the Space Needle has become a Seattle tradition.

starting at the bottom. The last lights at the top of the Needle are turned on exactly at midnight.

The height of the Space Needle has also attracted daredevils. In 1975, two parachutists made an unauthorized jump from the Space Needle's observation deck. Although those two were arrested, the Space Needle management saw the benefit of the publicity, and, later, in July 1976, a team of four parachutists jumped from the observation deck as part of a Space Needle promotion.

In 1982, major renovations were done to help keep the structure as modern as it seemed when it opened in 1962. As part of the renovations, a second restaurant was added at the 100-foot level. This

The silhouette of the Space Needle makes Seattle's skyline truly unique.

Did They Really Move the Space Needle?

In June 1987, the Space Needle "moved" 312 feet to the southwest. In 1987, the National Oceanic and Atmospheric Administration (NOAA) began a ten-year project to more accurately map the Earth using satellite technology. Part of their plan was to use prominent structures such as the Space Needle as benchmarks for the new maps. When the Space Needle's position was plotted using the extremely accurate information generated by the satellites high above the Earth, it was determined that the old maps were off by 312 feet. Therefore, the Space Needle appears to have moved on the new maps. They didn't really move the Space Needle!

establishment was received with mixed feelings by Seattle residents who were slow to accept changes in their city's symbol. In 1984, the 100-foot-level restaurant was made into a banquet facility.

In 1993, the elevators that climb up the outside of the central tower were replaced. The new cars look almost identical to the original golden capsules; however, they are much better. Not only are they faster and quieter with computer controls, they are also air-conditioned and have more glass so that young children can see out. When Otis Elevator selected the crew to do the elevator renovations, the man in charge was T. R. Kelly. Kelly had helped install the original elevators more than 30 years before.

The Space Needle is such an important part of Seattle that one TV station has installed a remote camera on top—its "eye in the sky." Any time there is something going on in Seattle, the view of it from the Space Needle can be included in the report. If the last 30-plus years are any indication, it can be expected that the Space Needle will continue to be special symbol for Seattle and the country well into the twenty-first century.

The Space Needle is sure
to remain an important
symbol of Seattle well into
the twenty-first century.

GLOSSARY

anchor bolt A large bolt used to attach a structure to its foundation.

beam The long, often I-shaped, pieces of steel used to build large structures.

butt weld The joining of the edges of two pieces of steel, by using heat or electricity to melt metal used as the adhesive.

cement A material made from lime and mixed with sand or gravel to make a substance that can be used to bond masonry material.

center of gravity The point at which an equal amount of an object's weight is above and below.

concrete A mixture of cement and sand or gravel that can be used to bond masonry together, or it can be poured into a form to create a solid structure.

crane A motorized device usually consisting of a steel tower and a series of pulleys, used to lift objects.

deed A legal document that describes the boundaries of a piece of property and declares who owns the property.

exposition A public show or fair.

flange The protruding edge of a beam or other object, often used to attach the object to another similar object.

foundation The underlying, often concrete part of a structure that supports the structure's upper part.

ingot A solid bar of metal that can be melted and formed.

iridium 90 A radioactive form of the metallic element iridium.

jig A mechanical pattern used to form an object to a specific shape.

power vibrator A machine that helps compact concrete as it is poured into forms.

prefabricate To assemble building materials before they are placed in their final position in a structure.

radiograph The process by which the image of an object is captured on film using radio waves. An X ray is the most common type of radiograph.

rebar (Contraction of *reinforcing bars*). The steel rods that are placed in concrete to make it stronger.

skip A small platform with low sides that is lifted by a crane on a construction site.

specifications The measurements and other information used to describe a structure's building materials, as well as the measurements of the structure itself.

sun louver A structural device used to limit the amount of sunlight that shines on a window.

welder A worker who is expert in the trade of joining pieces of metal together.

welding rod Metal rod of special compounds that is melted with electricity or gas flame to bond two pieces of metal together.

welding torch A device used to direct a very hot flame at the point that is to be welded.

CHRONOLOGY

1909 The Alaska-Yukon-Pacific Exposition is held in Seattle, Washington.

1954 A group of Seattle residents joins together to plan a celebration of the 50th anniversary of the Alsaka-Yukon-Pacific Exposition.

1955 Seattle voters approve $7.5 million for a fair.

Washington state legislature approves matching funds of $7.5 million for Seattle fair.

1956 March—City council appoints civic center advisory committee.

Civic Center Commission and fair organizers combine and decide to promote a larger fair.

Seattle voters approve a bond issue for a new civic center.

1959 September 9—U.S. Congress appropriates $9 million for a U.S. science pavillion at the Seattle World's Fair.

Idea for the Space Needle first discussed by fair organizers.

First drawings for the Space Needle shown to organizers.

October 1—Study recommends postponing the fair until 1962.

December 5—Space Needle plan shown to a large group of civic and community leaders including the governor of Washington.

1960 February—Fair president Joseph Gandy travels to Paris, France, and receives approval for a world's fair from the Bureau of International Expositions.

University of Washington

architecture professor Vic Steinbrueck is asked to assist in the design of the Space Needle.

Design for the Space Needle finalized.

1961 January 3—Land deal for the Space Needle finalized and land purchased from the city.

March—Banks agree to loan the money needed to construct the Space Needle.

March 8—Space Needle design approved.

March 30—Orders for the steel to build the Space Needle sent to U.S. Steel.

April 17—Excavation for the Space Needle's foundation begins.

May 22—Official ceremony marks the beginning of the construction of the Space Needle.

May 26—Foundation is poured in one day.

June—Steel erection begins.

September 1—Construction of the Space Needle reaches the 200-foot mark.

December 8—Steel erection is completed.

1962 April 20—Space Needle's last elevator arrives and is installed.

April 21—Seattle World's Fair opens and the Space Needle is in full operation.

October 21—The Seattle World's Fair closes; 2.75 million people have ridden to the top of the Space Needle.

1990 Goodwill Games held at Seattle Center.

1993 Space Needle elevators replaced.

FURTHER READING

Boring, Mel. *Incredible Constructions and the People Who Built Them.* New York: Walker & Co., 1985

Fowler, Allan. *World's Fairs and Expos.* Chicago: Childrens Press, 1991.

Loewen, N. *Seattle.* Vero Beach, Florida: Rourke, 1994.

Mansfield, Harold. *Space Needle USA.* Seattle, Washington: The Craftsman Press, 1962.

Morgan, Sally and Adrian Morgan. *Structures.* New York: Facts On File, 1993.

Snelson, Karin. *Seattle.* New York: Macmillan Children's Group, 1992.

SOURCE NOTES

Abbott, Walter M. "The Seattle World's Fair." *America,* September 15, 1962, 732.

"A.D. 1000 and Beyond." *New York Times,* September 17, 1961.

"After the Fair Is Over." *AIA Journal,* December 1972, vol. 58, 22–25.

"Aftermath in Seattle." *Harper,* February 1966, 22.

"Career Man of Fair: Joseph Edward Gandy." *New York Times,* April 13, 1962.

"Century 21 Postponed Until 1962." *Science,* October 30, 1959, vol. 130, 1170.

"Come to the Fair." *Time,* December 29, 1961, 13.

Davies, Lawrence. "Seattle Builds 1962 Fair." *New York Times,* September 17, 1961.

———. "Fair in Seattle to Open at Noon." *New York Times,* April 21, 1962, 42.

———. "Seattle Counts Its Fair Profits." *New York Times,* October 22, 1962.

Fun Facts and Anecdotes issued by the Space Needle, no date.

Judd, Ron. "Space Needle Gets a Lift but New, High-tech Elevator Cars Retain the Style that Elvis Knew." *Seattle Times,* June 15, 1993, A-1.

Lynes, Russell. "Seattle Will Never Be the Same . . ." *Harper,* July 1961, vol. 222, 20–25.

Morgan, Murray. "Seattle: Portrait of a Fair City." *New York Times Magazine,* April 15, 1962, 30.

"Needlemania: Towering Trivia and Tall Tales." *The Weekly,* no date, 43.

"100,000 at World's Fair." *New York Times,* September 17, 1962.

Patterson, Carolyn Bennett. "Seattle Fair Looks to the 21st Century." *National Geographic,* September 1963, 403–27.

"Seattle Rings up Century 21." *Newsweek,* March 26, 1962, 92–95.

"Seattle to Get First Monorail." *New York Times,* May 10, 1959.

"Seattle World's Fair 1962: April 21–October 21." *New York Times,* October 22, 1962, advertising supplement.

"Seattle Inherits a Science Center." *New York Times,* November 27, 1963.

"Seattle Set for World's Fair." *Iron Age,* May 4, 1961, 73.

"Seattle's Future." *New York Times,* April 7, 1963.

"Space Needle Structural Facts" issued by Space Needle, no date.

"Space Needle News: History in the Making" issued by the Space Needle, June 1990.

"Space Needle Trivia" issued by Space Needle, no date.

"Space Needle to Wear Medal During Games." *Seattle Times,* July 5, 1990, B-4.

"Space Needle Required 146,500 lb. of Weld Metal." *Welding Engineer,* May 1962, 47: 46+.

The Space Needle Story. Seattle, WA: Space Needle Corp. 1992, (Videotape).

"Startling World of Century 21." *Life,* May 4, 1962, vol. 52, 30–39.

Steinberg, Lynn. "2000: A Space Needle Odyssey: Here Comes the Party We've Waited a Thousand Years For." *Seattle Post-Intelligencer*, January 23, 1995, D-1.
"Symbol of World's Fair Is Dedicated at Seattle." *New York Times*, May 23, 1961.
"U.S. World Fairs Start Beating Their Drums." *Business Week*, April 22, 1961, 92.

INDEX